ALSO BY MOSAB ABU TOHA

Things You May Find Hidden in My Ear

Forest of Noise

Forest of Noise

Poems

MOSAB ABU TOHA

ALFRED A. KNOPF   New York

2024

www.aaknopf.com

Pages 79–80 constitute an extension of the copyright page.

Library of Congress Cataloging-in-Publication Data
Name: Abu Toha, Mosab, author.
Title: Forest of noise: poems / Mosab Abu Toha.
Other titles: Forest of noise (Compilation)
Description: First edition. | New York : Knopf, 2024. |
"This is a Borzoi book."
Identifiers: LCCN 2024019266 (print) | LCCN 2024019267 (ebook) |
ISBN 9780593803974 (hardcover) | ISBN 9780593803981 (ebook)
Subject: LCGFT: Poetry.
Classification: LCC PR9570.P343 A275 2024 (print) |
LCC PR9570.P343 (ebook)
LC record available at https://lccn.loc.gov/2024019266
LC ebook record available at https://lccn.loc.gov/2024019267

Jacket design by Arsh Raziuddin

Manufactured in the United States of America
First Edition

1st Printing

For my parents,
Awatef and Mostafa

Poetry is not a luxury.

—AUDRE LORDE

Every child in Gaza is me.
Every mother and father is me.
Every house is my heart.
Every tree is my leg.
Every plant is my arm.
Every flower is my eye.
Every hole in the earth
is my wound.

Contents

Younger than War   3

OBIT   5

Gaza Notebook (2021–2023)   6

My Dreams as a Child   11

My Son Throws a Blanket over My Daughter   13

Grandparents   15

My Grandfather's Well   16

No Art   18

We Are Looking for Palestine   19

You Came into My Dream   22

A Blank Postcard   23

The Last Kiss   24

Father's Myth   26

Palestinian Village   28

Thanks (on the Eve of My Twenty-Second Birthday)   29

Mothers and Mulberry Tree   30

My Library   31

This Is Me!   32

Under the Rubble   33

Daughter   37

The Ball and the Bombs   38

Gazan Family Letters, 2092   39

What a Gazan Should Do During an Israeli Air Strike   42

On Your Knees   43

Two Watches   49

See the Kites?   50

Request Letter   51

What a Gazan Mother Does During an Israeli Night Air Strike   52

Forest of Noise   53

History Class   54

1948   55

A Request   56

Love Poem   57

To My Mother, Staying in an UNRWA School Shelter
    in the Jabalia Camp   59

True or False: A Test by a Gazan Child   60

After Allen Ginsberg   61

After Walt Whitman   62

Mouth Still Open   63

Ramadan 2024   64

Rescue Plane   65

Howl   66

Icarus Falling   67

Who Has Seen the Wind?   68

Door on the Road   69

Right or Left!   70

Before I Sleep   71

Sunrise in Palestine   72

The Moon   73

For a Moment   74

Ash   75

This Is Not a Poem   76

Acknowledgments   79

Forest of Noise

Younger than War

Tanks roll through dust,
through eggplant fields.

Beds unmade, lightning in the sky, brother
jumping to the window to watch warplanes.

Clouds of smoke
after air strikes.

Warplanes: eagles
searching for a branch on which to perch.

No need for radio:
We are the news.

Ants' ears hurt with each bullet
fired from wrathful machine guns.

Soldiers advance, burn books.
Some smoke rolled sheets of yesterday's newspapers,

just like they did
when they were kids.

Our kids hide in the basement,
backs against concrete pillars,

heads between knees,
parents silent.

Humid down there
and the heat of burning bombs

adds to the slow death
of survival.

In September 2000,
I bought bread for dinner.

I saw a helicopter fire a rocket
into a tower,

concrete and glass
fell from high.

Loaves
of stale bread.

At the time,
I was seven:

decades younger than war,
a few years older than bombs.

OBIT

To the shadow I had left alone before I
crossed the border, my shadow that stayed
lonely and hid in the dark of the night,
freezing where it was, never needing a visa.
To my shadow that's been waiting for my return,
homeless except when I was walking by its side
in the summer light.
To my shadow that wishes to go to school
with the children of morning, but couldn't fit
through the classroom doors.
To my shadow that has caught cold now, that's been
sneezing and coughing, no one there saying to it *God bless!*
To my shadow that's been crushed by cars and vans,
its chest pierced by shrapnel and bullets
flying with no wings,
my shadow that no one's attending to,
           bleeding black blood
           through its memory
           now, and forever.

Gaza Notebook (2021–2023)

My two eyes, when closed,

see different things:
one me leaving Gaza in peace,
in one piece,
the other, me getting jailed at the Erez crossing point.
                    My head: a confused old TV channel
                        picking up crossed signals.

                    *

(In Egypt visiting the Red Sea)

Riding a jet boat for the first time,
my hat falls in the sea, waves
wear it now,

and at night I'm back home,
unable to sleep.

                    *

At fifth grade, I visit the school library.
On a wall by the door, a poster claims,
"If you read books, you live more than one life."
Now I'm thirty and whenever I look at faces
around me, old or young, on each forehead I read:
"If you live in Gaza,   you die several times."

                    *

The bomb when it pounded the sea
made an eye socket beneath the sand.
The fish thought the sea
had been crying forever.

*

She asked her teacher:
If there are four directions,
then why do we have only two feet?

*

When it rains, farmers think the sky loves them.
They are wrong. It rains either because
the clouds cannot carry the sacks of water too long,
or because a sparrow has said a prayer
when it heard the thirsty roots begging.

*

No one at *home.*

The doorknob   only dust touches it now.

Pots grow parched.
Frying pans miss the smell of olive oil.
Clotheslines everywhere pine for soap scent.
The flowerpot   the window   the key
the   [language].

*

stones of house after explosion   get amnesia

some forget they were in a wall in a bedroom or a kitchen or a bathroom
some in a ceiling
some forget they sat behind photo frames for years
a few stones   [forget]   they were stones
those hit   by the bomb

                          *

Birds draw the lines of their homes in the sky,
and the wind . . .

                          *

walking on the beach,
dreams grow between each two footprints
on the sand
                          and the waves . . .

                          *

Her dreams,
          she threw them onto the closest sea wave
          and that wave
                          never returned

                          *

Raindrops slide on windowpanes,
each one exploring a new space,
a bed made for the night,
or, on the kitchen counter, a glass full of water
                          (young ancestors)
                          (or missing siblings)

*

upon birth, mask up your children and leave them unnamed
                                                                    so
the angel of death can't find them

someone may ask
        why not paint their faces change their names
                        every day

a nightingale on the tree of dusk exclaims
        what if both the painter and the paint
                        work for the angel of death

a stone near a cemetery suggests
        why give birth to children
at all

                *

in the camp   house small
power off   humid
drone sounds buzz in through bullet holes
                                to have walls
                                is a blessing
outside
young and old
spend most of the night
in the street
                        in the camp

a street can become a living room
talking talking   watching cats and mice
scavenging through trash for cheese or meat
rooms inside: drawers for tired souls
temporarily stored

My Dreams as a Child

I still have dreams about
a room filled with toys
my mother always promised
we could have
if we were rich.
I still have dreams about
seeing the refugee camp
from a window on a plane.
I still have dreams about
seeing the animals
I learnt about in third grade:
elephant, giraffe, kangaroo,
and wolf.
I still have dreams about
running for miles
and miles with no border
blocking my feet,
with no unexploded bombs
scaring me off.
I still have dreams about
my favorite team playing
soccer on the beach,
me waiting for the ball
to come my way
and run away with it.
I dream still about
my grandfather, how much
I want to pick oranges
with him in Yaffa.

But my grandfather died,
Yaffa is occupied, and oranges
no longer grow
in his weeping groves.

My Son Throws a Blanket over My Daughter
Gaza, May 2021

At night, at home, we sit on the floor,
close to each other
far from the windows and the red
lights of bombs. Our backs bang on the walls
whenever the house shakes.
We stare at each other's faces,
scared yet *happy*
that, so far, our lives have been spared.

The walls wake up from their fitful sleep,
no arms to wipe at their bleary eyes.
Flies gather around the only lit ceiling lamp
for warmth in the bitter night,
cold except when missiles hit
and burn up houses and roads and trees.
The neighborhood next to us,
where Yazzan learned to ride his bike,
scorched.

Every time we hear a bomb
falling from an F-16 or an F-35,
our lives panic. Our lives freeze
somewhere in between, confused
where to head next:
a graveyard, a hospital,
a nightmare.
I keep my shivering hand
on my wristwatch,

ready to remove the battery
if needed.

My four-year-old daughter, Yaffa,
wearing a pink dress given to her by a friend,
hears a bomb explode. She gasps,
covers her mouth with her dress's ruffles.
Yazzan, her five-and-a-half-year-old brother,
grabs a blanket warmed by his sleepy body.
He lays the blanket on his sister.
You can hide now, he assures her.

Grandparents

In the refugee camp, Grandmother Khadra puffs away at her cigarette. Smoke mingles with the coffee steam rising from Grandfather Hasan's chipped but favorite cup. Short Khadra muses on her wedding party in Yaffa in 1946: *They placed two cinder blocks under my feet on the stage. My mother brought dinner for us at night: chicken soup, rice, and some bread she baked in her clay oven.*

Khadra turns to Hasan: *You lit the candle before the wind blew it out. Through our bedroom's wooden casement window, a breeze froze my makeup, but your kisses melted me down.*

Together in the refugee camp and thirty-five years after their wedding, Khadra fingers her beads while Hasan observes her from his wheelchair. Dust covers their photo frame, which Hasan hung on a wall when he could stand. Hasan's and Khadra's stories fill their small house. At night, it starts to drizzle, and beads of rain seep through some holes in their corrugated asbestos roof. Rain wakes my Khadra and her children. My father is still nine. Rain waters the stories that sleep on the old, tiled floor.

My Grandfather's Well

I never met Grandfather, but I can see him
close to a well in Yaffa. The forehead he's wiping
is a glittering, wrinkled map of the past.
His olive-wood cane leans
against an orange tree.

I can see birds the color of earth
when it rains.

I can watch them
harvest oranges, pile them
on roofs of houses
in the refugee camp.

Where have you been? Grandfather asks me,
his voice getting
weary of
plowing the thick, muddy
soil of language.
My arms are down, too tired to lift
even to say hi.

I've been pulling up buckets of water
from the camp's well,
searching for words
for my epic.

My grandfather stands still close to the well.
He never abandoned it, even after the Nakba,
even after death.
His hands pour water
down into the well.

In the refugee camp,
where land is strewn with
debris, where air chokes with rage,
my harvest is yet to arrive,
my seeds only sprout on this page.

No Art

The art of losing isn't hard to master.
—ELIZABETH BISHOP

You know everything will come to an end:
the sugar, the tea, the dried sage,
the water.
Just go to the market and restock.

Even your shadow will abandon you
when there is no light.
So just keep things that require only you:
the book of poems that only you can decipher,
the blank map of a country
whose cities and villages only you can recognize.

I've personally lost three friends to war,
a city to darkness, and a language to fear.
This was not easy to survive,
but survival proved necessary to master.
But of all things,
losing the only photo of my grandfather
under the rubble of my house
was a real disaster.

We Are Looking for Palestine

The sun rises and moves around.
It sets to visit other places.
And we, we are looking for Palestine.

The birds wake up and look for food.
They chirp on the blossoming trees, laden with fruit,
with peaches, apples, apricots, and oranges.
And we, we are looking for Palestine.

The sea waves lap against the shore.
They glitter and dance with the fishers' boats.
And we, we are looking for Palestine.

People travel to relatives and friends.
They book round-trip tickets, stuff their suitcases
with gifts and books and clothes.
And we, we are still looking for Palestine.

Sir, we have no airports and seaports;
no trains, or highways.
We have no passable roads, sir!
We *do* have crutches and wheelchairs.
Young men with one or no legs,
no longer able to work, as if there was work.

We travel to the West Bank or Egypt for surgery,
even to set a broken leg.
But we need a permit to enter.
We stuff our suitcases with pictures and memories.
They feel very heavy on the ground;

we can't carry them, neither can the roads.
They scar the surface of the earth.

We get lost in the past, present, and future.

When a child is born, we feel sad for him or her.
A child is born here to suffer, sir!

A mother feels the great pain in labor.
A child cries after leaving her dark place.

In Palestine, our dark is not safe.
In Palestine, children always cry.

If we want to travel, we leave many times.
In Gaza, you leave via either Erez or Rafah,
a hard escape to make,
so we search for the visa interview.
Cairo, Istanbul, Amman? (But not in Palestine!)

We don't have embassies, sir!
The one in Jerusalem is farther
than the Andromeda Galaxy.
Andromeda is 2.5 million light-years.
But our years stay heavy and dark.
It would take trillions of years.

Sir, we are not welcome anywhere.
Only cemeteries don't mind our bodies.

We no longer look for Palestine.
Our time is spent dying.
Soon, Palestine will search for us,
for our whispers, for our footsteps,
our fading pictures fallen off blown-up walls.

You Came into My Dream

A letter to my brother Hudayfah (2000–2016)

When you came, I paid no attention to your clothing, whether you
were holding something in your hand. A letter from There?
Are your hands still small? Could they carry a heavy letter written by
Fate? Fate, whose sharp fingernails scratch open my back's skin as it
misspells my name.

I knew I was dreaming. But why haven't I even conversed with you?
Maybe ask if you saw Grandfather up There? Maybe he is still stuck
and planted in Yaffa somewhere, tending an aging orange tree?
What kept my mouth from opening? (Silence makes my mouth sour.)
Was I put inside a glass medicine bottle on which They wrote not
"Keep out of reach of children," but "Keep silent in and out."
Who, what, are They?

Your sight was so fresh and sharp that I felt you could see through me,
into my bleeding past. I am crying, but my tears are cold. Tears are
falling on my feet, they burn the tiny, dark hairs on my toes. My feet
are bare. I have been walking for a long time, and the road is strewn
with the remains of my grandfather's bombed grave.

A Blank Postcard

To my brother Hudayfah (2000–2016)

I'm looking at the calendar. It's October 13. You died eight years ago. The square that besieges number 13 reminds me of a grave, the calendar page on the wall of a cemetery, the white wall of a shroud around Homeland, and my room a casket.

I still don't know where your grave is. I never looked for it, though the cemetery is a five-minute walk from home. Each time you come into my dreams is like getting a blank postcard. Maybe you're asking me to write you a letter? But where should I send it when no postman shows up on my street?

If it's comforting to you, I never stepped into the cemetery since you died. I used to pass by it on my way to the gym in my teens.

Now it's 2024, and the cemetery you were buried in was razed by Israeli bulldozers and tanks. How can I find you now?

Will my bones find yours after I die?

The Last Kiss

On the way to the battlefield

At the door of a train
heading to the next station
before the battlefield,
her hands wrap around the back
of his neck.

A soldier sits behind
or stands,
sending a goodbye
text to a relative.
Another checks
for the family photo
his mother put
in his inner jacket pocket.

The young wife
still at the door of the train
smells her husband,
smiles as she glimpses the lipstick
below his earlobe.
No textbooks or notebooks,
no pencils or erasers in his backpack.
Only toothpaste and a comb,
a few jet-black hairs from her,
a sandwich and a book of prayers,
a list of names
they both brainstormed
for the coming baby.

Around his neck, a scarf she bought him
on his thirtieth birthday.
Around his wrist

the watch he kept from school years.
She kisses him, his cap hides
her tearful eyes.
"The doors are shutting soon. Beware!"
A voice of an old man comes
through the train's speaker.

She never hears
the young man's voice again.

Father's Myth

My dad tunes the radio to a news station.
On the floor, I sit to do homework.
I'm in second grade.
My mother has been at Al-Nasr Children's Hospital
for three days.
My sister Asma' feels sick.
Asma' means *names*.
(She is dead now
but parents still give
names to their newborns.)

I was born in a refugee camp.

Our house is roofed with corrugated
tin sheets. Alleys in the neighborhood
too narrow for a father and a son
to walk beside each other.

My father once warned me,
If you dirty your clothes,
the sky will pour all its rain over you.
You'll become too sick to play outside for weeks.

One day, I play marbles with friends in the street.
I lose a game but refuse to give
my marbles away.
I flee down the bumpy, potholed roads,

trip over a stone other children used
as a goalpost. I dirty my clothes
with dust and mud.

I look up into the sky:
barely any clouds.

I arrive home, lunch on the table,
the same table I use to do homework.

Then—
a surprise storm tears open the sky;
the water tank on our roof
skids off its cinder blocks,
pounding the tin sheets.
It gets stuck between two metal rafters.

No one is harmed.
But the water pours
over me and my lunch
and my backpack.

The teakettle on the stove whistles
and my father smiles. He glances at my clothes,
wet mud as brown as my feet.

Later, friends outside call me
to play another game.

Palestinian Village

On the hill in the village, you can chock
the wheels of your vegetable cart
with a stone your grandfather once used
to crush thyme. Or smash garlic with a
stone your grandmother used as a doorstop.
You can lounge
on a wicker chair near a pomegranate tree,
where a canary never tires of singing.
You can dig a hole with your hands
and find an earthworm breathing
the freshness of soil revived by yesterday's rain.
You can make tea with sage or mint.
If a neighbor or a passerby smells it,
an invitation to join is extended.
You put more cups on your table,
you walk to the garden and pick
more fresh sage or more mint.

Thanks (on the Eve of My Twenty-Second Birthday)
After Yusef Komunyakaa

Thanks to my mother always, but
especially when she called for me
to join them at the table,
just seconds before shrapnel
cut through the window glass
where I stood watching distant air strikes.

My mother's voice, the magnet of my life,
swaying my head just in time.
Plumes of smoke choked the neighborhood.
It was night and when we ran into the street,
Mother forgot the cake in the oven,
the bomb smoke mixed with the burnt chocolate
and strawberry.

And thanks to the huge clock tower's bell
which saved my life. I was crossing the street
and my head, glued to my phone,
never heeded the honk of cars
or the wheels of vans
screeching onto the rough tarmac.
That bell tolled for me.
Sorry, Death, but it was the eve of my twenty-second birthday

and I had to be by the sea and listen to the lapping of waves,
the sound I last heard before my birth.

Mothers and Mulberry Tree

There is a dog giving birth to seven puppies

beneath a white mulberry tree under the clear night sky.
The dog groans with pain,
puppy after puppy cries, unaware where they are.

For them, it's still dark, whether in her belly or outside.
What country are we in?
That's not a question for a puppy to ask.

Only Mother dog and the soil beneath can hear
the branch of the mulberry tree—
for every moan
a blossom comes out.

From her bedroom window, a mother, still awake,
watches the dog, its puppies, and the mulberry tree,
while her child, eyes closed, suckles from her breast.

And the drone watches over all.

My Library

My books remain on the shelves as I left them last year,
but all the words have died.
I search for my favorite book,
Out of Place.
I find it lying lonely in a drawer,
next to the photo album and my old Nokia phone.

The pen inside the book is still intact,
but some ink drops have leaked.
Some words breathe its ink,
the pen like a ventilator
for a dozen patients:

Home, Jerusalem, the sea, Haifa,
the rock, the oranges, the sand,
the pigeon, Cairo, my mother,
Beirut, books, the rock, the sea, the sea.

This Is Me!

A city whose streets escaped it,
a house without windows,
a rain with no clouds,
a swimmer in the desert,
a shirt with ripped-off buttons,
a book with loose pages,
a lightless moon and colorless grass,
a toothless smile and suffocated laugh,
a dark painting on black canvas.
Do you understand?
I'm a table with no legs,
a noisy restaurant with no guests.
I write with an inkless pen.
I write my name in the air.
When I shout it, no voice comes out.

I look around and see many things,
but I see no one.

Under the Rubble

She slept on her bed,
never woke up again.
Her bed has become her grave,
a tomb beneath the ceiling of her room,
the ceiling a cenotaph.
No name, no year of birth,
no year of death, no epitaph.
Only blood and a smashed
picture frame in ruin
next to her.

*

In Jabalia Camp, a mother collects her daughter's
flesh in a piggy bank,
hoping to buy her a plot
on a river in a faraway land.

*

A group of mute people
were talking sign.
When a bomb fell,
they fell silent.

*

It rained again last night.
The new plant looked for
an umbrella in the garage.
The bombing got intense
and our house looked for
a shelter in the neighborhood.

*

I leave the door to my room open, so the words in my books,
the titles, and names of authors and publishers,
could flee when they hear the bombs.

*

I became homeless once but
the rubble of my city
covered the streets.

*

They could not find a stretcher
to carry your body. They put
you on a wooden door they found
under the rubble:

Your neighbors: a moving wall.

*

The scars on our children's faces
will look for you.
Our children's amputated legs
will run after you.

*

He left the house to buy some bread for his kids.
News of his death made it home,
but not the bread.
No bread.
Death sits to eat whoever remains of the kids.
No need for a table, no need for bread.

*

A father wakes up at night, sees
the random colors on the walls
drawn by his four-year-old daughter.

The colors are about four feet high.
Next year, they would be five.
But the painter has died
in an air strike.

There are no colors anymore.
There are no walls.

*

I changed the order of my books on the shelves.
Two days later, the war broke out.
Beware of changing the order of your books!

*

What are you thinking?
What thinking?
What you?
You?
Is there still you?

You there?

*

Where should people go? Should they
build a big ladder and go up?

But heaven has been blocked by the drones
and F-16s and the smoke of death.

*

My son asks me whether,
when we return to Gaza,
I could get him a puppy.
I say, "I promise, if we can find any."

I ask my son if he wishes to become
a pilot when he grows up.
He says he won't wish
to drop bombs on people and houses.

*

When we die, our souls leave our bodies,
take with them everything they loved
in our bedrooms: the perfume bottles,
the makeup, the necklaces, and the pens.
In Gaza, our bodies and rooms get crushed.
Nothing remains for the soul.
Even our souls,
they get stuck under the rubble for weeks.

Daughter

I ask her to remember,
not because I want to hear the story again,
but because I want to watch her face relive
the moment. That moment, her eyes sparkle with longing,
I can see how she flies from the tent
to a time when she leapt
through our farm in every direction with eyes closed,
only stopping at the fence, where our orange trees
embrace our neighbors' olive trees.
Some fallen oranges would tell her to open her eyes,
to pick them up and put them in a plate at our doorstep,
where children returning from school
would stop to gulp some.
I love the smell of oranges best
when she remembers.

The Ball and the Bombs

Gaza, July 16, 2014, boys from Baker family

children play soccer
on the beach   they are eight
eight bombs thump the field   four kids killed
four wounded   without checking his watch
the referee announces   a draw (4–4)
       he knows the game
should be over   [unless there are more   planes   more bombs

        more goals]   the audience
       the waves
         nobody cheers
   an ambulance worker
sees the ball the kids used   the soccer ball [unharmed]
the referee blows   a second final whistle
       on the smashed scoreboard
       (the kids' team wins)

Gazan Family Letters, 2092

1

Children feel petrified at night. Power outages most of the time.
Grandfather has not left his room for seventeen days. It all occurred
when he looked at himself in the mirror. He could not believe he'd
aged that much. Grandfather began to count the hairs on his head.
Everything was white. We waited at his door outside and smelled
something woody burning in his room. White and brownish smoke
sneaked from beneath his old door. It was his cane.

2

Doves perch on the roof of our hen coop, guzzle water from rain
puddles. In the neighborhood, ducks and hens pick at what the wind
has carried and laid on the earth: a seed, or a dried leaf, or a piece
from a newspaper soaked in a child's urine. Universities closed for a
long time. Warplanes have damaged all roads, especially leading to
hospitals. Mother still reads Quran every day and fasts on Mondays
and Thursdays. Father plants cucumber and tomato seeds, while
Mother watches through the door, muttering prayers hoping the seeds
will sprout soon. Mother and Father usually share with neighbors
what grows in the little garden.
And the neighbors pray, too.

3

As usual, our baby slowly opens the fridge door in the morning,
grabs whatever he can carry in his small hands. He ambles down the
stairs, sits in Grandma's lap in the garden, then plays with the hose
Grandpa uses to water his newly planted flowers. Did I tell you about
his new flower plants? Damask rose, orchid, aster, black-eyed Susan,
calendula, and marigold.
Our baby (he turns three next month) walks to our neighbor's house,
peeks inside to see which of the kids are awake so he can share what

he has in his small hands. Everyone's still asleep. He returns home and waits until he hears the school bus. Out through the window, he watches the kids as they get off the bus. He walks down again and starts to mess with their bags.

4

Our neighbors sold their house. They loaded their furniture and books onto a truck, but left the portrait of their grandfather hanging on the living room wall. I asked the old wheelchaired man, "Why did you do that?" He said, "If we removed it, the whole house would crumble."

5

My older brother has traveled to Europe to search for work. He is a bodybuilder. My brother has found a job. He now cleans streets and shops. Someone once asked him, "Why do you clean streets better than shops?" He said, "Because it's where I sometimes have to sleep!"

6

I'm sorry I couldn't send a letter for yesterday. I had trouble finding paper to write on, and I later realized my seven-year-old son had used up all of it. He had a dream the other day and tried a bunch of times to draw what he saw. He said it was a castle on the Mediterranean, but there was no water in the sea. A Coleridge of our bleak time.

7

I've been seeing a young man in our neighborhood dragging a suitcase. He's never traveled before, and I think he doesn't have the means to. I was told he lost his family in an air strike.
I felt curious enough to ask him, "What's inside your suitcase? It seems heavy. Why do you take it out with you every day?"

"I'm training myself to not miss my plane if I had to travel. I never experienced such a thing. Inside my suitcase are some clothes of my father, mother, two sisters, and three brothers. I also have their shoes and slippers. The suitcase is their new home and I want to put it in a safe place. And I also have my father's favorite books, mainly poetry books and short stories. He never had the chance to finish a novel. You know, wars and work."

I looked around us and I could see the roads marred by the wheels of his suitcase. His house still remains a heap of rubble, like a fallen tent made of ragged cloth.

What a Gazan Should Do
During an Israeli Air Strike

Turn off the lights in every room / sit in the inner hallway of the house
/ away from the windows / stay away from the stove / stop thinking
about making black tea / have a bottle of water nearby / big enough
to cool down / children's fear / get a child's kindergarten backpack
and stuff / tiny toys and whatever amount of money there is / and the
ID cards / and photos of late grandparents, aunts, or uncles / and the
grandparents' wedding invitation that's been kept for a long time /
and if you are a farmer, you should put some strawberry seeds / in one
pocket / and some soil from / the balcony flowerpot in the other / and
hold on tight / to whatever number there was / on the cake / from the
last birthday.

On Your Knees

I'm wearing a backpack.
It has my kids' winter clothes.
I'm carrying my three-year-old child in one arm.
He was born in Boston.
In my second hand, I raise our passports.
My wife and our two other kids
stroll ahead.

*

Yaffa is thirsty,
Yazzan raises the white flag.
Mostafa in my arm gets tired,
wishes to be back with his grandmother.
A soldier calls out to me
by describing what I'm carrying.

*

I'm nameless for the first time.
I'm stateless for a long time.
I don't know what time it is
right now.

*

Guns pointed at me.
A gust of wind.
The tank behind.
Artillery shelling in the distance.
Drop your boy,
drop everything!

I'm not a thing,
I will not drop myself.

*

On your knees!
A new soldier calls me by my full name.
He even says my grandfather's name.
I love the name of my grandfather.
I hate the soldier,
I hate his name,
which I do not know.
Your ID number, say it aloud!
Remove your clothes,
even your boxer shorts.
Turn around.

*

In my ears, I'm hiding
my mother's stories,
my father's recitation
of the Holy Quran when I am sick,
the sound of my childhood alarm clock ringing
when I open my eyes for school.

*

On your knees!
How many passports do you have?
Stay on your knees!

My son's American passport,
my Palestinian passport,
my two other kids' passports.

We were going to the Rafah Border Crossing, I say.

Shut the f*** up!
On your knees!

UNRWA.

On your knees!

Yes, I'm a teacher, I say.

On your knees!

But I won't reach the blackboard
when on my knees.
I'm handcuffed, blindfolded.
I'm shoved from the back of my neck.

On your knees!
Terrorist!
On your knees!

Show me any proof, I ask.
A slap across my face.

You get us proof!
On your knees!

It begins to rain.
My teeth chatter.

On your knees!

Someone next to me weeps,
I need to be with my pregnant wife
and baby daughter.

On your knees!

We *are* on our knees.

On your knees!

They throw us into a truck.
It travels and travels
and then stops.
They take us out.

On your knees!

Minutes later, someone
kicks me in the stomach.
I fly with pain.

On your knees!

Then someone kicks me in the face.
My head is down.
My nose bleeds.

On your knees!

I hear soldiers chitchatting.

On your knees!

They take us far away from Gaza,
to the Negev desert,
someone there tells us:

On your knees!

Most of the men with me
are sleeping outside of Gaza
for the first time.

On your knees.

In the toilet, no toilet paper,
no water to clean.

You are done?
On your knees!

Drops of water, a piece of bread.

On your knees!

Interrogation. Two hours later
a soldier in English says,

We are sorry about the mistake.
You are going back to Gaza

on your knees.

Two Watches

He's wearing two watches,
one set to the local time in New York,
the other to Gaza's.

In a café with friends,
waiting for his tea at the round green table,
whenever his eyes fall
on the Gaza dial, he remembers the kids
of his neighborhood running in the alleys,
girls playing hopscotch, boys playing soccer.

At night, when the light in the Gaza watch doesn't work,
he knows electricity is off in his neighborhood.
If the metal case grows warm,
he knows bombs have started to fall.

If the watch doesn't move, he knows
a relative, a neighbor, a friend, has died.
When that happens, the watch won't work again
until their body is buried.

But what if there is no body anymore?

He is happy to have time, a watch that works.
He is happy to have time.

See the Kites?

There is a little moon
in the dark sky over Gaza.
The moon is made of kites.

Now it grows bigger—more kites,
shining over Gaza,
protecting her children as they try
to sleep through bombs and screams
in the laps of their mothers' souls.

Request Letter

He pens a quick letter on paper (a letter as plain in regard to form as possible, with no white spaces) and throws it in the graveyard at night:

Angel of death,
When you collect the souls of those killed in an air strike, do you mind leaving a sign for us, so we know who is who? Because last time my old kindergarten teacher couldn't recognize her daughter's face, which ear or arm or bloody finger on the dusty streets was hers. And a father wouldn't recognize which was his child if it wasn't for the size of shoes (28 European size still on the sole) that he bought her for the new school year.

On the back of the paper, he pens the same letter in Arabic, because who could know what language the angel of death uses, the most-spoken language in the world, or the language of God:

إلى ملك الموت،

عندما تجمعُ أرواحَ من قُتلوا في الغارة الجوية، هل تُمانع بأن تتركَ إشارةً تدلنا على من هو من؟ لأنه في المرة الماضية لم تستطع معلمتي الكبيرة أيام الروضة أن تتعرف على وجه ابنتها، أيّةُ أذنٍ أو ذراعٍ أو أصبع مدمي في الشارع المغبر كان لابنتها. وكذا أبٌ لم يستطع أن يعرف أيّة طفلةٍ كانت ابنتَه لولا حجمُ الحذاء (٢٨ بالمقياس الأوروبي كان منقوشاً على نعل الحذاء) الذي اشتراه لها للعام الدراسي الجديد.

What a Gazan Mother Does During
an Israeli Night Air Strike

She gathers all her kids around
in her bed, as one collects and packs
books and clothes before leaving a hotel.
She counts her kids' ears, mouths, noses, then
looks into their eyes. And, I swear, she smiles.
She sings a night song to bury in the ground the sound of bombs,
to disappear the whirring of drones back into the clouds.

She hugs each child, still here,
after every bomb and,
if she knows a bomb is about to light up the sky and the room,
she covers her kids' eyes and
loudly asks,
What can you see when your eyes are closed?
hoping her trembling voice may hide
the bomb's eradicating sound.

Forest of Noise

A car slides on our asphalt street,
like an iron running on an ironing board.
But in my city, streets are never flat.
Potholes from bombs are everywhere,
like crows' nests in a forest of noise.

History Class

At my first history class,
the only students attending
are the future, the present, and the past.
But when I step in, the future gets ready to leave,
while the past is handcuffing the present,
slicing its hamstrings,
and dyeing its clothes gray.

1948

Nakba, the year when Israel was founded after expelling 800,000
Palestinians and destroying 530 villages

bullet   bomb
smoke   dark
    door locked
                          stay with me daddy
                                stay inside
it's calm outside for a second
smoke   dark
outside   mice scamper between   children's feet
running on a   trembling road
hens   and bullets   food still on plates
on deserted kitchen tables
water warmed   screams everywhere
roller coaster   broken   coffee spilt
on rug grandmother sewed   cat dead   kittens
mewing   sparrow on window   shrapnel hits door
water leaks   earth soaks blood
fighters aim at   soldiers shielded inside armored vehicles
one falls   another springs to   fall again
in blood pool
bombs   smoke chokes   morning   air
lips drenched   sun helpless   moon   absent
no oil for lamp   a surviving lamb bleats
                                  on hill
and hundreds of tongues in the village no sound

A Request

After Refaat Alareer

If I am going to die,
let it be a clean death.
No rubble over my corpse,
no broken dishes or glasses,
and not many cuts in my head or chest.
Leave my ironed untouched jackets
and pants in the closet,
so I may wear some of them again
at the funeral.

Love Poem

To Maram

When I sit to write,
you know that
and you distract our kids
from my writing room.

When I read the poem to you
and ask, *What do you think?*
You say, *It's beautiful,*
though you know
that frustrates me.

Beautiful is not enough,
not next to you,
not next to the poem.

I'm asking you about
what makes my poem a poem,
just like when you ask me
what makes you my love:

your tears, your scolds when I spend
too much time writing my poems,

when the tea grows cold,
your jealousy of the poem,

the way you searched for me
when I was kidnapped
(our daughter, Yaffa, told me
all about it when I returned),

how I searched for you all—

your carrying our home, our destroyed home,
with you in your memories
(I forget so quickly
and that's why I take a lot of photos),

your hand holding the pencil with me
when my fingers freeze out of fear,
your name,
which reminds me there is a goal.

To My Mother, Staying in an UNRWA School Shelter in the Jabalia Camp

I lost contact with my mother on December 2, 2023, while I was on my way to Egypt with my wife and three kids. I was able to hear my mother's voice only after over a month.

Do you still lie on your mattress
reading from the Holy Quran
to calm yourself down?
Do you still use your reading glasses
or have the F-16s and the smoke of their bombs
blinded your small eyes?
Do you still drink your morning coffee
with Dad, or have you run out of cooking gas?
Do you still know how to make my favorite cake?
Last month was my thirty-first birthday. You promised
to make me cake on the rubble
of our bombed house,
though I had told you many times,
It is no longer a house.
You just glared at me, sucked your teeth.
I need you, Mother. You are my better heart
when I feel I am about to die.
I do not know
if you are even alive.

True or False: A Test by a Gazan Child

To the West

1. Palestine was empty of people before 1948.
2. Gazans can travel whenever they wish.
3. A father in Gaza can afford to take his child to a hospital and even to pay for a grave if his child is dead.
4. Gaza has an airport but not a seaport.
5. All people in Gaza come originally from Gaza.
6. If dolphins do not show up near the shore, Gaza's children ask their parents to sail them to the sea to meet the lazy dolphins.
7. Every day one can hear airliners crossing the sky over Gaza.
8. Parents take their children to parks every month.
9. Schools in Gaza are open for students to learn, not shelter in.
10. People in the West Bank and Gaza can invite each other over for a meal.
11. Our aunt and her family in Jordan can visit us in Gaza, or we can visit them.
12. The only things that fall from the sky in Gaza are rain and bird poop.

Note:
When you finish with answering the questions, hand the test to any Palestinian child and they will be able to grade it for you. Plus, they can sign your book for me on my behalf.

After Allen Ginsberg

I saw the best minds of *my* generation destroyed in a tent,
looking for water and diapers for kids;
destroyed by bombs;
a generation under the rubble
of their bombed houses;

I saw the best brains of *my* generation
protruding from their slashed heads.

After Walt Whitman

I become grass in America, if you want me,
look for me under your boot-soles.
I become a child in Gaza, if you want me,
look for me under the rubble of our house.

Mouth Still Open

Someone's mouth is still open. He hadn't finished yawning
when shrapnel
pierced
through
his chest,
stung his
heart.
No wind
could
stop the
flying pieces
of shrapnel. Even
the sparrow on the lemon tree nearby wondered how they

     could

            move

               with

           no

    wings.

Ramadan 2024

Around that dinner table, missing are the chairs
where my mother, my father,
and my little sister used to sit with us on Fridays,
and where my siblings and their kids
used to drink tea at sunset when they visited.
No one is here anymore. Not even the sunset.
In the kitchen, the table is missing.
In the house, the kitchen is missing.
In the house, the house is missing.

Only rubble stays, waiting for a sunrise.

Rescue Plane

I wish I had a rescue plane
to fly over Gaza
to drop wheat flour and tea bags,
tomatoes and cucumbers,
to remove the rubble of the houses,
to retrieve the corpses of my loved ones.

I wish for a second rescue plane
to drop flowers for children—
the ones still alive—to plant
on the graves of their parents and siblings
in the streets or schoolyards.

The wish behind the wish?

I wish there were no planes at all.
I wish there were no war.
I wish we never had to wish.

Howl

I'm howling, howling
in Cairo.

I jump off my chair. I hug
the closest thing to me,
the gray corner of my room,
my head glued to it like
a stamp so eager to travel.
Books on the shelf,
they listen to the whispers of my nose
as it smells the old paint,
as it searches for the fingers of the mason
beneath the paint.

My nose hears the mason's radio
playing Om Koulthoum
and news about the *Uprising* nearby.
My nose smells the burning tires and stones
thrown by young hands.

I open my eyes to the image of my mother
on my phone
handing me oranges she picked
from a tree that's now under the rubble,
but still howling
in the wind.

Icarus Falling

According to Brueghel in 2023
Icarus did not fall in the sea.
He got hit by a bomb
or a tank shell.
Shrapnel scattered his body
over the ruins of bombed houses

and schools and museums.
There was no plough-man
but the strawberries and grass
continued to grow, and the dogs
and cats under the moonlight
scavenged piles of corpses.
No one heard the pieces of shrapnel falling
in the sea or the drones' buzzing sound.

Who Has Seen the Wind?

After Bob Kaufman

The ceiling of my bedroom, my fridge
and the stale bread in it,
the notebook inside which I hid the love letters
from my wife before we married,
the foreign coins in my piggy bank,
my expired debit cards
and my brother's death certificate,

little pieces of shrapnel in or near
each of these.

Door on the Road

In the Refugee Camp,
after the explosion, a door flies into a far street,
rests near a heap of rubble.

Clouds of dust settle on the coughing
neighboring houses—
their noses swollen by the heat
of the scorched air.
A girl passes by, sees the bleeding door, opens it. A corpse
lies beneath.
The earth weeps. Though some fingers got cut,
the dead young man still clutches in his hand
a very old key—the only thing he's inherited
from his father. It's the key to their house
in Yaffa. He was sure it's been destroyed, but the key
will be his passport to Yaffa when they return.
Now, neither he nor their knocked-down house in the Refugee
Camp can stand.
The girl closes the door. Windows of tears
open in her heart.

Right or Left!

Under the rubble,
her body has remained
for days
and days.
When the war ends,
we try to remove
the rubble,
stone
after stone.

We only find one small bone
from her body.
It is a bone
from her arm.
Right or left?
It does not matter
as long as we cannot
find the henna
from her neighbors' wedding
on her skin,
or the ink
from a school pen
on a little index finger.

Before I Sleep

Before I sleep,
Death is always
sitting on my windowsill,
whether in Gaza or Cairo.

Even when I lived
in a tent,
it never failed
to create a window
for itself.

It looks me in the eye
and recounts to me
the many times
it let me live.

When I respond, "But you
took my loved ones away!"
it swallows the light in the tent
and hides in the dark to visit next day.

Sunrise in Palestine

The smoke of bombs
dropped from F-16s
has covered the city's sky.

Fighters smuggle the sunlight
through tunnels
beneath our houses.

The Moon

She's lying on the asphalt.
Her small belly, her chest,
her forehead, her hands,
her cold feet bare in the night.
A hungry cat paces.
Shrapnel rings
as it hits neighboring
houses already bombed.
The hungry cat sees the girl,
her wounds still warm.
Hungrier.
The girl's father lies next to her
on his back. The backpack he wears
still has the girl's favorite candy
and a small toy.
The girl was waiting
till they arrived
to eat her lollipop.
The cat gets close
to try the flesh;
a bomb pounds the street.
No flesh, no girl,
no father, no cat.
Nobody is hungry.

The moon overhead
is not the moon.

For a Moment

Her small body rides in my arms
as I run to the hospital.
There is no electricity
and the inner hallways are
a forest lined with cots.
The girl I carry
is dead,
I know that.
The pressure of the explosion
tore apart her thin veins.
I know she is dead,
but everyone who sees us
runs after us.
You are alive
for a moment,
when living people
run after you.

Ash

We are skidding off the map.
We make a hole in the air
as we fall.
The air is stuffed with ash
each time an F-16 drops
its bombs on cemeteries.

This Is Not a Poem

It's vacant here except for hundreds of stone boxes
and a yellow, dry floor of sand.
Even birds find no trees to perch on.
Inside each box, two hands,
or maybe one,
or maybe no hands; one leg, two legs,
or maybe no legs; a head, or none; a chest,
or a smashed one;
or nothing at all.
All of the body parts
we learned about at school or touched
on our loved ones.
A box may perfectly fit the size of a corpse.
It may be bigger. Or it could just be empty.

Grandfather, I don't know where yours is,
but your wheelchair is surely nowhere inside
any of these boxes. You need nothing
to help you move now.

Brother, I know you're sleeping in one,
but I never searched for it.
Your loud snoring once
directed me to your bed. But not anymore.
I cannot tell if they've inscribed your name
on the gravestone. Not sure if there's
a gravestone, or if you're still in your grave,
or where you watch us from,

watch me
writing this.
But what is this?

This is not a poem.
This is a grave, not
beneath the soil of Homeland,
but above a flat, light white
rag of paper.

Acknowledgments

I would like to thank the editors and staff of the following magazines and journals where some of the poems in this collection were first published:

The New Yorker: "OBIT"

Los Angeles Review of Books: "Gaza Notebook (2021–2023)"

The New York Review of Books: "What a Gazan Should Do During an Israeli Air Strike," "The Moon"

The Café Review: "Clouds, Smoke, Alarm Away from Gaza," "You Came into My Dream," "Thanks," "The Last Kiss," "This Is Not a Poem"

Ploughshares: "Two Watches," "Sunrise in Palestine," "History Class"

Poetry London: "Request Letter"

The Atlantic: "Younger than War"

The Nation: "Gazan Family Letters, 2092"

The Progressive: "My Dreams as a Child," "My Son Throws a Blanket over My Daughter," "What A Gazan Mother Does During an Israeli Night Air Strike"

Solstice Literary Magazine: "We Are Looking for Palestine"

The Poetry Review: "On Your Knees"

AGNI: "This is Me!," "For A Moment"

Democracy in Exile: "Door on the Road"

Mondoweiss: "My Grandfather's Well"

The Paris Review: "My Library"

Poets.org: "Mouth Still Open"

Liberties Journal of Culture and Politics: "Howl," "Who Has Seen the Wind?,"
"Right or Left!," "Rescue Plane," "No Art"

Special gratitude to Kaveh Akbar, Refaat Alareer (RIP), Marouf Al-Ashqar
(RIP), Ammiel Alcalay, Mona Awad, Diana Buttu, Elise Crosby, Jonathan
Dee, Stephen Greenblatt, Daniel Gross, Brooks Haxton, Richard Hoffman,
Mary Karr, Christopher Kennedy, Askold Melnyczuk, Naomi Nye, David
Remnick, Bruce Smith, Dana Spiotta, Judith Thurman, and Jane Unrue for their
friendship, support, and belief in me and my work.

Deepest gratitude, again, to Mary Karr and Kaveh Akbar for offering to read the
manuscript first and provide their insights.

My deepest thanks to the Scholars at Risk Program at Harvard, the Lannan
Foundation, and Syracuse University for their invaluable support to me and my
small family during these dark times.

To Elaine Katzenberger and Stacey Lewis at City Lights, publisher of my first
book: I love you so, so much. You gave me more than I would ask for.

I'm grateful to my editor at Knopf, John Freeman, and the remarkable team who
worked with me on this book with enthusiasm, care, and love.

To my literary agent, Eric Simonoff: I'm thankful to you for carrying my work
with you and placing it in the right hands.

To my wife, Maram, and our children, Yazzan, Yaffa, and Mostafa: Without you
none of these poems would survive.

To my parents, Awatef and Mostafa, and my siblings, Aya, Mohammad, Asma'
(RIP), Hamza, Hudayfah (RIP), Sondos, Afnan, and Saja, and all their children:
May you survive to read this. May I sign you copies of this book in Gaza soon.
I wish my words would turn into clouds that could protect you and all our
neighbors and friends from the bombs.

To the souls who remain stuck under the rubble of their houses for weeks or
blocked by clouds of smoke from continuing the journey.

To Gaza, I will continue to search for my books under your rubble, for my
shadows in your bombed streets and fields of corn and strawberry, and for
humanity in your razed graveyards.